The Planet Promise
I promise to:

Rethink what I use and buy.
Refuse what I don't need.
Reduce my waste and carbon footprint.
Reuse things when I can.
Recycle as much as I can.
Rot food in a <u>compost bin</u>.
Repair broken things.

Earth's Eco-Warriors are going green for good! But what does it mean to "go green"? Earth has a certain amount of <u>natural resources</u> that we use to do almost everything. "Going green" means living in a <u>sustainable</u> way. We need to think about how we can reduce our carbon footprints to help the <u>environment</u>.

www.littlebluehousebooks.com

Copyright © 2025 by Little Blue House, Mendota Heights, MN 55120. All rights reserved. No part of this book may be reproduced or utilized in any form or by any means without written permission from the publisher.

Little Blue House is distributed by North Star Editions: sales@northstareditions.com | 888-417-0195

Library of Congress Control Number: 2024936701

ISBN
979-8-89359-004-3 (hardcover)
979-8-89359-014-2 (paperback)
979-8-89359-034-0 (ebook pdf)
979-8-89359-024-1 (hosted ebook)

Printed in the United States of America
Mankato, MN
082024

Eco-words that look like <u>this</u> are explained on page 24.

WE ARE EARTH'S ECO-WARRIORS

Are you an Eco-Warrior? Greta, Bailey, and Pietro are Earth's Eco-Warriors! Eco-Warriors care about the environment. They made the Planet Promise and are trying to save planet Earth.

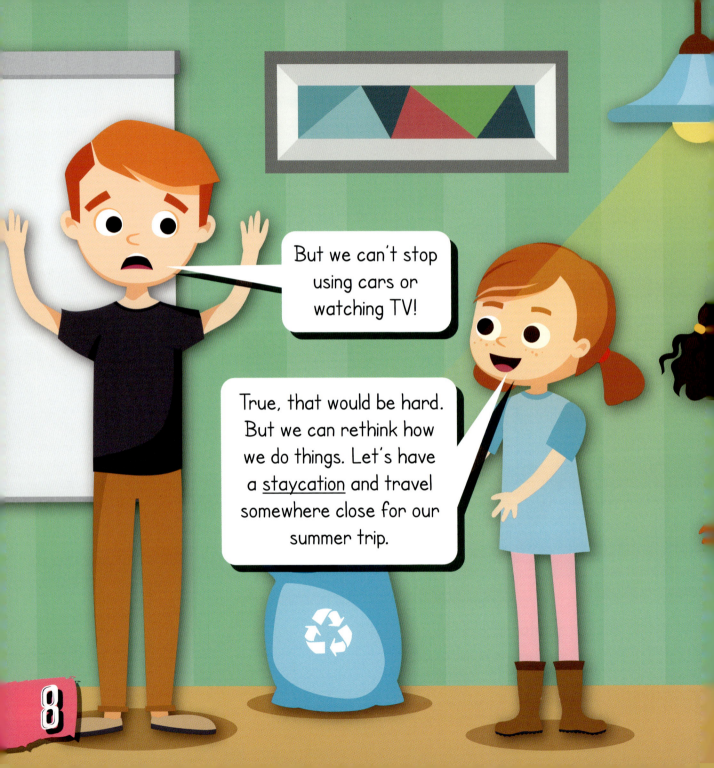

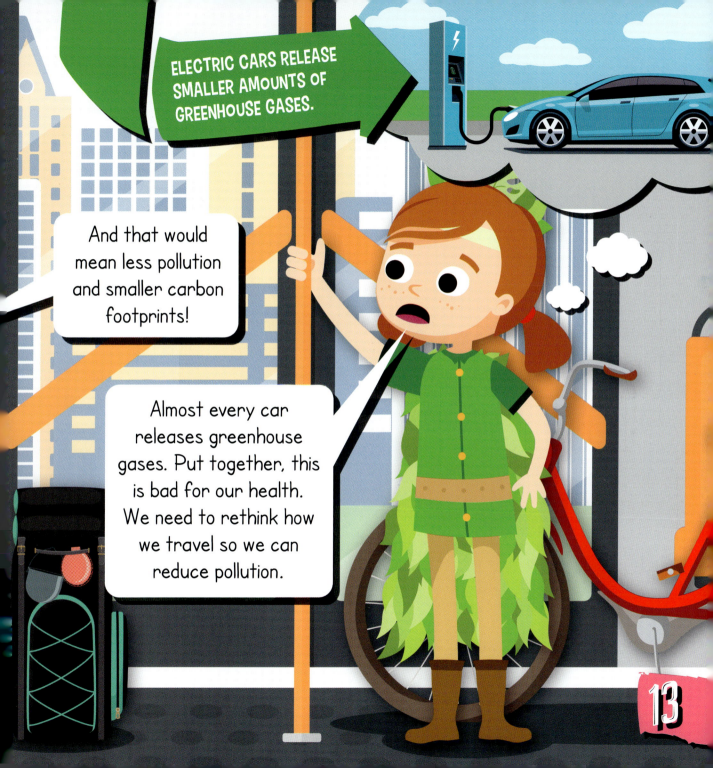

REDUCING CARBON FOOTPRINTS

The next day, Pietro showed his parents more ways to reduce their carbon footprints. He showed them a website. People who are looking to make up for the size of their carbon footprints can visit the website and give money to projects all over the world.

THIS IS CALLED CARBON OFFSETTING.

Some projects plant trees, and others help people rethink how they live. Would you like to find out more about carbon offsetting?

Visit this website to figure out your carbon footprint:

FOOTPRINT.WWF.ORG.UK

Learn more about carbon offsetting on this website:

CARBONFOOTPRINT.COM/OFFSETSHOP.HTML

ECO-WORDS

atmosphere	The mixture of gases that make up the air and surround Earth.
carbon offsetting	Making up for the size of your carbon footprint by giving money to projects that lower the amount of carbon in the atmosphere.
compost bin	A special bin where yard waste and some food scraps turn into soil.
crude oil	A liquid that is found underneath the ground and is used as a fuel.
energy	A type of power, such as light or heat, that can be used to do something.
environment	The natural world.
fuel	Something that can be used to make energy or power something.
greenhouse gases	Gases in the atmosphere that trap the sun's heat.
natural resources	Useful materials that are created by nature.
pollution	Harmful and poisonous things being added to an environment.
renewable	Not able to run out.
standby	A mode where something looks like it is turned off but still uses energy.
staycation	Going on vacation close to home.
sustainable	Done in a way that doesn't harm the environment or use up Earth's natural resources.
turbines	Machines that make energy by using flowing materials such as air or water to turn blades.

INDEX

airplanes, 5
animals, 15, 17
bicycles, 9, 11, 21
carbon dioxide, 5–7, 12
carbon footprints, 2, 6, 9, 11, 13, 19–20, 22–23
energy, 10, 18–19, 21
litter, 15, 18
oil, 16–17
Planet Promise, 2–3, 14
pollution, 5, 13
turbines, 18

PHOTO CREDITS

Cover & Throughout – Olga1818, Bukavik, Lorelyn Medina, 2&3 – GenerationClash, 4&5 – Igogosha, Bukavik, Tartila, 6&7 – piggu, Oliver Hoffmann, KittyVector, Inspiring, robuart, 8&9 – HappyPictures, Elvetica, 10&11 – CandyDuck, Anatolir, Sergey Mastepanov, Malinovskaya Yulia, intararit, 12&13 – Visual Generation, Kitty Vector, petovarga, 14&15 – aliaksei kruhlenia, the8monkey, 16&17 – Maquiadora, intararit, 20&21 – Diana Vasileva, 22&23 – Amanita Silvicora.

Images are courtesy of Shutterstock.com. With thanks to Getty Images, Thinkstock Photo, and iStockphoto.

All facts, statistics, web addresses, and URLs in this book were verified as valid and accurate at the time of writing. No responsibility for any changes to external websites or references can be accepted by either the author or the publisher.